ADELE

ADELE
MUSIC MEGASTAR

LESLIE HOLLERAN

LERNER PUBLICATIONS ◆ MINNEAPOLIS

Lerner Publications Company
An imprint of Lerner Publishing Group, Inc.
241 First Avenue North
Minneapolis, MN 55401 USA

For reading levels and more information, look up this title at www.lernerbooks.com.

Image Credits: Gareth Cattermole/Getty Images, Cover, p.40; Editor1000/Wikipedia Commons PD, p.13; Matt Sayles/Invision/AP, p.1; REUTERS/Mario Anzuoni/Alamy, p.6; Michael Tran/FilmMagic/Getty Images, p.8; Pete Still/Redferns/Getty Images, p.10; JMEnternational/Getty Images, pp.11, 22, 39; House Of Fame LLC/Michael Ochs Archive/Getty Images, p.15; Panther Media GmbH /Alamy Stock Photo, p.17; PA Images /Alamy Stock Photo, p.18; PA Images / Alamy Stock Photo, p.20; Kevin Mazur/WireImage/Getty Images, pp. 21, 30; Yui Mok/PA Images/Getty Images, p.23; Kevin Winter/Getty Images, p.24; Jennifer Graylock/FilmMagic/Getty Images, p.26; Lane Turner/The Boston Globe/Getty Images, p.28; Dave M. Benett/Getty Images, p.29; Quarterflash/Vantage News/AP, p.31; PA Images / Alamy Stock Photo, p.32; Ron Sachs/Pool/Getty Images, p.33; Sascha Steinbach/Getty Images, pp.35, 36; Cliff Lipson/CBS/Getty Images, p.37; Tom Cooper/Getty Images, p.38.

Main body text set in Rotis Serif Std 55 Regular. Typeface provided by Adobe Systems.

Library of Congress Cataloging-in-Publication Data

Names: Holleran, Leslie, author.
Title: Adele : music megastar / Leslie Holleran.
Description: Minneapolis, MN : Lerner Publications, 2023. | Series: Gateway biographies |
    Includes bibliographical references and index. | Audience: Ages 9–14 | Audience: Grades 4–6
    | Summary: "Adele is known for her emotional songs and powerful voice. With 15 Grammy
    awards, Adele is rolling in the deep with praise. Learn more about Adele's rise to frame, what
    inspires the singer-songwriter, and more"– Provided by publisher.
Identifiers: LCCN 2022023301 (print) | LCCN 2022023302 (ebook) | ISBN 9781728476582
    (library binding) | ISBN 9781728486345 (paperback) | ISBN 9781728482781 (ebook)
Subjects: LCSH: Adele, 1988-–Juvenile literature. | Singers–England–Biography–Juvenile
    literature.
Classification: LCC ML3930.A165 H65 2023 (print) | LCC ML3930.A165 (ebook) | DDC
    782.42164092 [B]–dc23/eng/20220517

LC record available at https://lccn.loc.gov/2022023301
LC ebook record available at https://lccn.loc.gov/2022023302

Manufactured in the United States of America
1-52239-50679-8/10/2022

CONTENTS

UK Born and Bred   9

Brixton Blues   12

Finding Her Voice   14

Phenomenal Rise   16

Making a Debut   20

On a Roll   25

Whirlwind World Tour   30

30 and Beyond   37

Important Dates   42

Source Notes   44

Selected Bibliography   46

Further Reading   47

Index   48

Adele sings at the 2012 Grammy Awards.

British singer-songwriter Adele Adkins was getting ready to perform at the Grammy Awards on February 12, 2012. Thirty-nine million people were watching on TV. Interest in the ceremony was unusually high. Rapper LL Cool J was hosting, and pop icon and six-time Grammy winner Whitney Houston had died unexpectedly the day before.

Adele had released her album *21* in 2011. It was the world's best-selling album of the year. Adele had also been nominated for six awards, including Album of the Year and Best Pop Solo Performance. The only female artist to win six awards in one year was singer-songwriter Beyoncé. She had won six Grammy Awards in 2010. Could Adele match such an incredible winning record?

The state of Adele's voice added to the suspense. She had undergone throat surgery a few months earlier. People were undoubtedly wondering: Would the voice they loved to listen to sound as it did before?

It was a huge moment for Adele.

Adele holds up her six Grammys.

She won the award for Best Pop Solo Performance for her hit song "Someone Like You." While accepting the award, she thanked both her co-songwriter, Dan Wilson, and her team of doctors. She said that they had brought her voice back.

After winning four awards that evening, she sang "Rolling in the Deep," another hit from *21*. She began with the chorus and sang it without musical instruments to show her powerful voice. Soon the entire auditorium was clapping along with her. When it was over, she received a standing ovation.

The final award of the evening was Album of the Year. Adele's *21* won. She had won each award she was nominated for, tying Beyoncé's record of six Grammys. After her final win of the night, Adele said to her mom, watching at home in London, "Your girl did good. Mom, I love you." It was an understatement, but Adele has remained relatable as she rises to the top. Her fans adore her for it—for being someone like them.

UK Born and Bred

Adele Laurie Blue Adkins was born on May 5, 1988, in London, England. Her parents are Penny Adkins from London and Mark Evans from Wales. Like England, Wales is part of the United Kingdom (UK). Adkins and Evans never married. They dated until they broke up when Adele was very young. Evans eventually returned to Wales, where his parents lived.

The artistic Adkins raised Adele. They lived in a two-bedroom flat in Tottenham, a diverse neighborhood in North London. Adele and her mom were part of a large and supportive family. Adkins's parents, four siblings, and nieces and nephews lived nearby. Adele had thirteen cousins to play with. Adele also visited her father and his parents, John and Rose Evans. They lived three hours away in Cardiff, the capital of Wales. Adele spent many of her summers there.

As a fan of contemporary music, Adkins went to concerts in London. She wanted Adele to share these experiences and brought her along. After turning five, Adele went with her mom to a one-day pop music festival, Great Xpectations, in Finsbury Park. One of Adkins's favorite groups, the Cure, was headlining. At a young age, Adele got to see and hear live performances because of her mom.

Adele also watched musicians perform on television. Adkins would let Adele stay up late on Friday nights to watch *Later . . . with Jools Holland*. The weekly show featured new and established performers.

The Cure is an English rock band. It formed in 1978 and has had different members over the years.

The Spice Girls perform at a British award show in 1998.

At about eight years old, Adele loved listening to pop music. One of her favorite groups was the Spice Girls, a British girl group with five singers. The Spice Girls released their first record-breaking No. 1 hit, a catchy song called "Wannabe," in July 1996. Adele was inspired by Geri Halliwell, also known as Ginger Spice. She said, "I'm going to do that. I want to be Ginger Spice."

Adele didn't just listen to the Spice Girls. She listened to all the popular pop artists. Some of her favorites were the Backstreet Boys, Britney Spears, Destiny's Child, and Take That, a very popular British boy band. The Queen of Pop, Beyoncé, was a member of Destiny's Child before she launched a solo career.

When Adele was nine, she and her mom left the familiarity of Tottenham. First, they moved to Brighton on the south coast of England 54 miles (87 km) from

London. Then, when Adkins began dating someone, she and Adele moved to Brixton in South London. Adele would spend her middle school years at Chestnut Grove Academy in South London, which was on the opposite side of the River Thames from where she grew up.

Brixton Blues

Adele struggled in middle school. She wasn't receiving support for her musical interests. She wanted to sing and perform but didn't receive any encouragement from her teachers. Adele was required to take clarinet lessons to become part of the choir. The requirement may have seemed unnecessary, but learning to play the clarinet would help her later in an important audition.

After school, Adele hung out with friends at a nearby park. On the playground, she staged Destiny's Child sing-offs with her friends.

Adele knew that she wanted to become a professional musician. Her mom encouraged her to try out for *Pop Idol*. This television show picked the best young singer in the UK. Two seasons aired from 2001 to 2003. But Adele was only thirteen in 2001 and too young to audition. *Pop Idol* contestants had to be at least sixteen.

One night, Adele was singing at home while her mom's friend was visiting. The friend, a singer, was impressed by Adele's voice. She encouraged Adele, and it made her believe she could become a singer too.

The BRIT school teaches students many art forms, including music, digital design, and film.

Soon after, Adele learned about the British Record Industry Trust (BRIT) School for Performing Arts & Technology. At first she wasn't interested in attending. She planned to make it on her own. But when she learned she could leave Chestnut Grove Academy if the BRIT School accepted her, she decided to apply.

Founded in 1991, the BRIT School is public but receives money from Britain's music industry. It's the only tuition-free performing arts school in England. Equipment, rehearsal rooms, and musical instruments are free as well. As a vocational school, the BRIT School prepares students for a range of careers in the arts. Music industry careers include singer-songwriter, producer, composer, musician, teacher, and sound engineer.

To apply, Adele had to fill out an application and audition. She was one of a couple of hundred students competing for twenty-four spots in 2002. In her application, Adele described herself as someone who would "keep trying until I am completely satisfied with what I have created." She also mentioned that she wanted to explore arranging music and different music styles. She played a short piece, "Tumbledown Blues," on the clarinet and sang the song "Free" by Stevie Wonder for her audition.

BRIT School music director Liz Penney watched Adele audition and was amazed by her voice. Penney thought to herself, "Well, that's a larger voice than you would expect from a thirteen-year-old."

Adele was accepted! She would receive the training she needed for a career in music while finishing school.

Finding Her Voice

Adele spent most of her first two years at BRIT completing her math and English classes. She only had one day a week to focus on music. But she made the most of it by writing lyrics, singing, and playing the guitar. Adele was finding where she belonged. She befriended a theater student named Laura Dockrill. The pair loved vintage clothes and dangling earrings. Adele and Laura became best friends.

Adele was happy to be at BRIT. Years later, she said, "It was really inspiring to wake up every day to go to

Etta James sang a variety of genres including blues, jazz, rock and roll, and soul.

school with kids that actually wanted to be productive at something and wanted to *be* somebody."

Around this time, Adele came across the music of American singers Ella Fitzgerald and Etta James in a record store. The store was selling old records at two for five pounds, the money used in the UK. Using her allowance, Adele bought an album by each artist. Fitzgerald was known as the Queen of Jazz. James was mostly a rhythm, blues, and soul artist. Adele didn't listen to the records right away or even soon after. When she finally did, three years later, she was tremendously inspired. She found the kind of music she wanted to sing in these two famous voices, especially James's. Years later, Adele said, "I taught myself how to sing by listening to them."

In her third and fourth years at BRIT, Adele was able to focus on music. She composed songs, recorded them in the school's studio, and performed live.

An argument with her mom about her plans for her future led Adele to compose "Hometown Glory." It's one of the first songs she wrote and shared publicly. Adkins wanted her to go to a university in Liverpool, but Adele did not want to leave London. In a matter of minutes, Adele put her thoughts on paper and wrote lyrics for a song describing her love of London. She performed "Hometown Glory" for her mom and told her this is why she was staying. The song served its purpose. Adkins stopped trying to get her to go to Liverpool.

Creating a demo tape of her songs was a requirement for graduation. So, Adele recorded "Hometown Glory," "Daydreamer," and "My Same." "My Same" was about her friendship with Laura Dockrill. She let a classmate post her demo on MySpace, a social media site. She thought that the best that might come of the post would be an internship. But it would lead to much more.

Phenomenal Rise

The year 2006 was a big one for Adele. In May she turned eighteen and graduated from high school. At her final BRIT concert, she sang "Daydreamer." Her song had just placed third in the school's annual songwriting competition.

MySpace is a social media website that began in 2003.

Someone at a record label heard Adele's recordings on MySpace. Impressed by her music, a representative from XL Recordings, an independent British record label, reached out to Adele. The company wanted to sign her and produce her albums.

But Adele didn't have a manager. A manager could help her with the business side of singing and songwriting. A manager negotiates contracts, advocates for their clients with record labels and producers, and handles tour schedules. Managers and artists typically

Adele plays a gig in 2007.

have close working relationships. Adele contacted Jonathan Dickins, a manager who XL Recordings had recommended. The two met and decided to work together. A few months later, Dickins negotiated a contract between her and XL Recordings.

As she worked on songs for her album, Adele lined up performances at London clubs. She befriended artists who let her play at their shows. Her first public performance was in August.

At these early gigs, Adele played her three original songs and would sometimes cover Etta James's "Fool That I Am." She strummed her acoustic guitar as she sang.

Adele remembered one of her first performances. The room was hot and packed. Then she started to sing. "The whole room was silent, and I saw these random girls just, like, crying," Adele said. "There's nothing more freeing than playing live, nothing." Adele saw the impact her music had on people. She wanted to keep performing and engaging with audiences.

Carefully Chosen Covers

Adele typically performs her own music, but she also covers other musicians' songs. For her first album, Dickins suggested Adele cover Bob Dylan's "Make You Feel My Love." She listened to the song and decided to include it. "It's about regretting not being with someone, and it's beautiful," she said. "It's weird that my [favorite] song on my album is a cover, but I couldn't not put it on there."

For 21, Adele covered the Cure's "Lovesong." Her mother was a big fan of the British group. Adkins had taken Adele to see the Cure perform when she was just five years old. Adele has said that the Cure provided "the soundtrack to [her] early life."

Adele performs a concert in 2008.

Making a Debut

By early 2007, Adele had a fourth song for her album. She was struggling to write more, but then she and her boyfriend broke up. Adele used her feelings about the relationship ending to write eight more songs.

Adele worked with producers and musicians to perfect her songs. Her album was named *19* because she was nineteen when she wrote most of the songs. Describing her album, Adele said, "So there's pop; there's a bit of electro; there's jazz; there's folk; and of course there's SOUL. . . . You know, the album genuinely did just come together very naturally and very organically."

Before her record was released, Adele was invited to be a guest on *Later . . . with Jools Holland*, the weekly music show she grew up watching. Adele sang "Daydreamer" and "Hometown Glory."

Former Beatles star Paul McCartney was also on the show that night. Adele wanted to talk with McCartney after the show but was too nervous. Instead, he stopped her. McCartney's thoughtfulness brought Adele to tears.

Adele and Paul McCartney smile together at the 2012 Grammys.

Adele is interviewed before attending a 2008 award show.

Adele released *19* and her single "Chasing Pavements" in January 2008 in the UK. Her album topped the UK charts and sold a half million copies. "Chasing Pavements" hit No. 2 on the singles charts. The album was a success in the UK, and Adele wanted to bring it to the US. Her first US show was at Joe's Pub in New York City in March. The show was planned so US music executives could hear her sing. XL Recordings' executives were hoping to make a deal with a US company to distribute Adele's music in America. The executives were impressed, and Columbia Records offered her a deal. The next night in her dressing room before a show, Adele signed the contract with Columbia Records. Then a tour of the US and Canada was arranged for 2008 where Adele would perform at fourteen different locations.

In October 2008, Adele appeared on the late-night television show *Saturday Night Live (SNL)*. People were particularly interested in the show because of an appearance by a vice-presidential candidate, Sarah Palin, and *SNL*'s comedic election coverage. Seventeen million viewers were tuned in when Adele sang "Chasing Pavements" and "Cold Shoulder." Adele had the chance to meet Rick Rubin, then cochair of Columbia Records and a famous record producer, at the *SNL* filming. He had flown in from California for the occasion.

SNL had its largest viewership in fourteen years that night. Adele called it the night that changed her life. Before that night, *19* was No. 40 on the iTunes chart. The next morning, it had risen to No. 8. By the time her plane landed in London later that day, it was No. 1.

Adele sings in London in 2008.

Adele accepts her award for Best Female Pop Vocal Performance in 2009.

On February 8, 2009, Adele attended the Grammy Awards for the first time. She had been nominated for four Grammys. She won Best New Artist and Best Female Pop Vocal Performance. The Jonas Brothers were expected to win Best New Artist, but she beat them. In her acceptance speech, she thanked several people: her manager, Jonathan Dickins; her mom, friends, and family; and her US and UK record labels, XL and Columbia. She sang "Chasing Pavements," the song that had earned her the Best Female Pop Vocal Performance Grammy.

Back at her hotel after the Grammys, she met Ryan Tedder, a singer and songwriter. Tedder has his own group, OneRepublic, and has also helped create hits for other well-known pop stars, including Taylor Swift and Ariana Grande. Tedder saw Adele get into an elevator and joined her. The two began talking and promised to be in touch soon. They made plans to work together on Adele's next album.

On a Roll

Adele's tour for *19* ran from 2008 to 2009. The shows, An Evening with Adele, were in North America and Europe. She canceled summer tour dates in the US to spend time with a boyfriend. She later regretted the decision. But their relationship and breakup provided a lot of material for her next album. She began working on it once the tour ended.

Explaining why she writes songs, Adele said, "Songs are how I feel, and that is the only way I do get it out of me. It's for me, for my own peace of mind. In reality I can't really admit things to myself so I have to put it in a song."

Adele first worked on a few new songs with London producer and songwriter Paul Epworth. They cowrote "Rolling in the Deep" in one day. The track they recorded ended up on the album. Epworth said, "She had had her heart broken, and she was in pieces, and you can really hear that—her anger and her sadness. Sometimes I just don't think you can re-create that or fake it." Epworth and Adele wrote two other songs for her album. She thought about naming the album after "Rolling in the Deep" but decided on *21*. It was her age when she made

In 2013 Adele and Epworth hold up an award they won for a song they wrote together.

the record and matched how she titled her first album.

In spring 2010, Adele recorded more of *21* at Rick Rubin's California studios. While there, Adele also reconnected with Ryan Tedder and met with songwriter Dan Wilson. Tedder and Adele cowrote "Rumour Has It" and "Turning Tables." Adele recorded "Rumour Has It" in one take. Dan Wilson collaborated on "Someone Like You." The song consists only of her voice and Wilson playing the piano. It was one of the last songs to be produced and was the last track on the album.

After finishing *21*, Adele went on the Adele Live tour in 2011. A couple months into the tour, Adele was doing a sound check before a show in Minneapolis, Minnesota, when she lost her voice. She saw a doctor who diagnosed her with acute laryngitis. The condition affected her voice box. Her vocal cords, the smooth muscles that vibrate to produce sound, were irritated. She went to Denver, Colorado, but had difficulty singing. So, she canceled additional shows in the US to rest her voice and went home to England to recover. Adele returned to the US and made up the canceled dates in August.

Inventive Language

Adele used metaphor and British expressions in her songs "Chasing Pavements" and "Rolling in the Deep." British people call sidewalks pavements. By chasing pavements, Adele meant she was running along the sidewalk, but not after someone or something. It was a metaphor for the hopeless relationship she was in. When Adele sang the song for a US television audience in 2008, she changed the final mention of "pavements" to "sidewalks" to help viewers understand.

"Rolling in the Deep" comes from the British expression "roll deep." It means you can trust someone. In "Rolling in the Deep," Adele sings about how she and her boyfriend could have had a strong relationship and "roll deep." But he didn't feel as strongly as Adele did, so they would never be that close.

Massachusetts General Hospital has special lasers that can stop vocal cord bleeding.

Adele's problems with her voice would soon start up again. She was supposed to be back on tour in the US in the fall. But a more serious problem with her voice developed. She had a vocal cord hemorrhage. Her vocal cords were bruised from excessive strain. Her doctor said it was a common condition among singers.

In October Adele had laser vocal cord surgery at Massachusetts General Hospital in Boston. Her doctor repaired the hemorrhage. After surgery, she was not allowed to speak for weeks so her vocal cords could heal. They not only healed, but her voice got better. She could hit notes she couldn't reach before.

Life was looking up for Adele. Nearly eighteen million copies of *21* were sold in 2011. She sang at the 2012 Grammys with the audience cheering her on.

BRIT Awards

The BRIT Awards is an annual celebration of the biggest musical stars in the UK. Musicians perform their greatest hits at the BRITs. Money from the event supports charitable causes, such as the BRIT School, where Adele trained in music. Her album *21* won British Album of the Year in 2012. As of 2022, she has won twelve BRIT Awards.

Adele performs at the 2011 BRIT Awards.

Whirlwind World Tour

After the 2012 Grammys, Adele stepped out of the spotlight. She was dating a British man, Simon Konecki. She had met Konecki in 2011. Konecki founded Drop4Drop, a charity bringing clean water solutions to communities in need of them.

Adele and Konecki attend the Grammy Awards in 2013.

Adele carries her son, Angelo, through an airport in 2015.

In late June, she announced that she was pregnant. Her message said, "I'm delighted to announce that Simon and I are expecting our first child together. I wanted you to hear the news direct from me. Obviously we're over the moon and very excited."

Adele gave birth to a son, Angelo, on October 19, 2012, but did not issue a public statement. She has been extremely protective of her son's privacy. She and Konecki filed a lawsuit on Angelo's behalf when photos of milestone baby moments appeared in the media in 2013. These moments included his first family outing and going to a playgroup. Adele and Konecki claimed his right to privacy was violated and won the suit.

Royal Recognition

In 2013 the British royal family honored Adele for her musical contributions. Prince Charles, Queen Elizabeth's eldest son, made Adele a member of the Most Excellent Order of the British Empire and gave her a medal during a ceremony at Buckingham Palace, the queen's home. The monarchy launched the order over one hundred years ago to recognize civilian and military accomplishments during World War I (1914–1918). It awards accomplishments in the arts, sciences, and public service and for humanitarian efforts.

After the event, Adele said, "It was an honor to be recognized and a very proud moment to be awarded alongside such wonderful and inspirational people."

Adele and Prince Charles shake hands in 2013.

On February 24, 2013, Adele attended the Academy Awards. She and Epworth had written a song, "Skyfall," for the twenty-third James Bond film. Their song won an Oscar.

Adele began creating her third album. She continued to work with some of her *21* collaborators but also looked for new ones. She worked with best-selling music artist Bruno Mars and record producer Greg Kurstin.

Adele and Kurstin began working on the song "Hello" in 2014. They wrote the verses first. Then several months later, they wrote the chorus. At the time, Adele was busy with her toddler son. They finished the song in 2015. The song helped Adele create the rest of the album.

Bruno Mars is an award-winning singer-songwriter.

"Hello" was released in October 2015 before the album came out. The album, called *25*, named once again for her age when she worked on it, came out in November 2015. It had been three years since she had released new music. Fans waited eagerly for its release.

"Hello" became Adele's second No. 1 hit single on the UK charts. It debuted at the top of the iTunes chart in eighty-five countries. Other popular songs on the album were "Send My Love (To Your New Lover)" and "When We Were Young." The final song on the album, "Sweetest Devotion," was inspired by her relationship with her son, Angelo.

"Skyfall"

In 2011 producers of the James Bond film *Skyfall* asked Adele to write the theme song. James Bond films feature a fictional British secret agent. Adele read the entire script before agreeing to write the song. She asked Paul Epworth to work with her. The two created the song "Skyfall." He composed the music, and she wrote the lyrics. "Skyfall" was recorded at the legendary Abbey Road Studios in London, made famous by the Beatles. For the recording, a seventy-seven-piece orchestra and choir accompanied Adele's powerful voice. The song won an Academy Award, the first ever given to a Bond theme song.

Adele smiles while performing in 2015.

Adele's previous albums were breakup records, and she described *25* as a makeup record. "I'm making up with myself," Adele said. "*25* is about getting to know who I've become without [realizing]." Adele was learning who she was as a person and a musician.

In 2016 she went on a 123-concert world tour. The tour kicked off in Belfast, Northern Ireland, and was supposed to end with four shows at Wembley Stadium in London the next year. The tour was arranged so that when Adele's son began school, Adele, Konecki, and Angelo would be home. But she wasn't able to perform all four final shows. With just two shows left, her voice gave out.

Adele sings passionately in 2015.

In a heartfelt statement to fans on Twitter, she apologized for canceling the final two shows. She said, "The last two nights at Wembley have been the biggest and best shows of my life. To come home to such a response after so long away doing something I never thought I could pull off but did has blown me away. However, I've struggled vocally both nights. . . ." She then explained that she had seen her doctor and that damage to her vocal cords made her incapable of singing. It was a difficult end to a lengthy tour for her and her fans. She was learning that her voice had limits to how much and often she could perform.

30 and Beyond

In 2018 Adele married Konecki in a private ceremony. Soon Adele realized that she was unhappy in the marriage even though Konecki was a great father to their son. She said, "I definitely chose the perfect person to have my child with. That—after making a lot of knee-jerk reactions—is one of my proudest things I've ever done." She filed for divorce in 2019. Angelo was six years old. It was hard for him to understand his parents divorcing. Adele began writing songs to explain what was happening.

Adele had a television special on November 14, 2021, just a few days before her fourth album, *30,* came out.

Adele sings during her 2021 television special.

Oprah is known for her interviewing skills.

The two-hour show included an interview with Oprah Winfrey filmed before the concert in Oprah's rose garden. Adele discussed her divorce in detail. The centerpiece of the special was the concert. It was at sunset at the Griffith Observatory in Los Angeles. She sang her hits and new songs. Angelo attended—it was his first time seeing his mom perform for an audience.

Adele released *30* on November 19, 2021. Its initial sales didn't come near *25*'s, but *30* was still the world's best-selling record of 2021. Record sales for all artists have been declining over the past few years. More people are streaming albums digitally through a service instead of buying them. For example, in 2021, 274.5 million people streamed Adele's *30* on Spotify, but only 1.5 million purchased the album.

Adele was excited for her 2022 Las Vegas, Nevada, residency. She would perform a show there for twelve weeks from January to March. Fans from all over were planning to see her. But the COVID-19 virus spread among her team, making half of them sick and unable to work. And supplies needed for the show had not arrived in time. The show wasn't living up to her artistic standards. Adele decided to cancel the residency with short notice instead of putting on shows she wasn't proud of. She was very apologetic. Some fans were understanding while others were disappointed.

She returned to London for the BRIT Awards in early February and took home three awards that evening.

Adele poses with a trophy at the 2022 BRIT Awards.

Adele sings at the 2022 BRIT Awards.

One was for Album of the Year for *30*. She dedicated the win to Angelo and Konecki. She talked about how patient Angelo had been with her over the years. She thanked London record producer Inflo, a new collaborator. He had worked with her on three songs for *30* and was also a 2022 BRIT Award recipient. Her second win was for Song of the Year for "Easy on Me." And she won Artist of the Year.

She directed her acceptance speech for Artist of the Year to the next generation of artists. She said, "We have so many incredible, new, young artists coming up and never lose sight of why you are who you are. The reason people are into you is because of something you have in you. Don't ever let go of that, ever."

At the beginning of July, Adele performed two shows at Hyde Park in central London as part of a British Summer Time concert series. Sixty-five thousand people gathered each night to hear her perform. These were her first public concerts since her 2017 Adele Live tour. She choked up as she began "Hello" on the first night and interrupted the song to say, "I'm so happy to be here!" It was an emotional homecoming.

Adele excels at turning her emotions and experiences into art. Heartache, friendship, and motherhood have inspired her songs. Her powerful voice brings her songs to life. Adele is a global phenomenon, and her fans can't wait to see what she does next.

IMPORTANT DATES

1988   Adele Laurie Blue Adkins is born to Penny Adkins and Mark Evans on May 5 in London.

2006   Adele graduates from the BRIT School, a school for the performing arts, in London.

She signs with XL Recordings, an independent British record label, in September.

2008   Her debut album, *19*, is released.

2009   Adele receives two Grammy Awards, one for Best New Artist and the other for Best Female Pop Vocal Performance.

2011   Her second album, *21*, is released in January.

She undergoes throat surgery in Boston, Massachusetts.

2012   She wins six Grammy Awards for *21*.

She gives birth to a son, Angelo.

2016   Her third album, *25*, comes out.

She goes on her first world tour and completes 121 of 123 scheduled dates before her voice gives out.

2018   She marries Simon Konecki, Angelo's father.

2019   She files for divorce from Konecki.

2021   She releases her fourth album, *30*.

2022   She cancels her first residency in Las Vegas due to illness among her team and delivery delays caused by the COVID-19 pandemic.

She wins three BRIT Awards.

SOURCE NOTES

9   "Adele Sweeps the Grammy Awards," NPR, February 13, 2012, https://www.npr.org/transcripts/146786971.

11   Sean Smith, *Adele* (London Harper, 2017), 25.

14   Smith, 40.

14   Smith, 42.

14–15   Smith, 45.

15   "Adele before She Was 'Rolling,'" interview, Hits Daily Double, December 22, 2011, https://hitsdailydouble.com/news&tid =280854&title=ADELE-BEFORE-SHE-WAS-FAMOUS.

19   Hamish Bowles, "Adele: Feeling Groovy," *Vogue*, April 2, 2009, https://www.vogue.com/article/adele-feeling-groovy.

19   Caroline Sullivan, *Adele: The Stories behind the Songs* (London: Carlton Books, 2018), 66.

19   Sullivan, 126.

20–21   Pete Lewis, "Adele: Up Close and Personal," interview, Blues and Soul, July 4, 2008, http://www.bluesandsoul.com/feature /302/the_futures_looking_rosie_for_adele/.

25   Smith, 102.

25   James C. McKinley Jr. "Hot Tracks, the Collaborative Method," *New York Times*, February 9, 2012, https://www.nytimes.com /2012/02/10/arts/music/paul-epworth-on-producing-adele.html.

31   Reuters staff, "British Singer Adele Is Pregnant with First Child," Reuters, June 29, 2012, https://www.reuters.com/article /entertainment-us-adele-pregnant/british-singer-adele-is -pregnant-with-first-child-idUSBRE85S1BJ20120629.

32 Jessica Derschowitz, "Adele Received Royal Honor at Buckingham Palace," CBS, December 19, 2013, https://www.cbsnews.com /news/adele-receives-royal-honor-at-buckingham-palace/.

35 Caroline Sullivan, *Adele*, 141.

36 Nicola Slawson, "Adele: Singer 'Devasted' after Voice Troubles Force Her to Axe Wembley Shows," *Guardian* (London), July 1, 2017, https://www.theguardian.com/music/2017/jul/01/adele -devastated-after-voice-troubles-force-her-to-axe-wembley -shows#:~:text=Adele%20has%20said%20she%20is,last %20concerts%20of%20the%20year.

37 Giles Hattersley, "Adele, Reborn: The British Icon Gets Candid about Divorce, Body Image, Romance & Her 'Self-Redemption' Record," *Vogue*, October 7, 2021, https://www.vogue.co.uk/arts -and-lifestyle/article/adele-british-vogue-interview.

41 Rhian Daly, "Adele Says 'Not Many People' Make 'Personal' Albums Anymore at BRITs 2022," NME, February 8, 2022, https://www.nme.com/news/music/adele-not-many-people -make-personal-albums-anymore-brits-2022-3157030.

41 Mark Sutherland, "Adele Dazzles at Homecoming Concert in Hyde Park: 'London, I Love You so Much,'" *Variety*, June 1, 2022, https://variety.com/2022/music/reviews/adele-london -hyde-park-concert-review-1235308231/.

SELECTED BIBLIOGRAPHY

Bowles, Hamish. "Adele: Feeling Groovy." *Vogue*, April 2, 2009. https://www.vogue.com/article/adele-feeling-groovy.

Gompertz, Will. "Adele: The Full Story." BBC, February 26, 2016. https://www.bbc.com/news/magazine-35152397.

Horton, Adrian. "Weight Loss, Deadlifts and Divorce: What We Learned from Adele's One Night Only Special." *Guardian* (US edition), November 15, 2021. https://www.theguardian.com/music/2021/nov /15/weight-loss-deadlifts-and-divorce-what-we-learned-from-adeles -tv-special.

Lewis, Pete. "Adele: Up Close and Personal." *Blues and Soul,* July 4, 2008. http://www.bluesandsoul.com/feature/302/the_futures_looking _rosie_for_adele/.

McKinley, James C., Jr. "Hot Tracks, the Collaborative Method." *New York Times*, February 9, 2012. https://www.nytimes.com/2012 /02/10/arts/music/paul-epworth-on-producing-adele.html.

Shapiro, Marc. *Adele: The Biography*. New York: St. Martin's, 2012.

Shaw, Lucas. "Adele's Worst-Selling Album Is Still the Year's Biggest Record." *Bloomberg*, January 25, 2022. https://www.bloomberg.com /graphics/pop-star-ranking/2022-january/adele-s-worst-selling -album-is-still-the-year-s-biggest-record.html.

Smith, Sean. *Adele*. London: Harper, 2017.

Sullivan, Caroline. *Adele: The Stories behind the Songs*. London: Carlton Books, 2018.

Vinter, Robyn. "Spotify Hides Shuffle Button after Adele Says Albums Should 'Tell a Story.'" *Guardian* (US edition), November 21, 2021. https://www.theguardian.com/music/2021/nov/21/spotify-hides -shuffle-button-adele-albums-should-tell-a-story.

FURTHER READING

Billboard: Adele
    https://www.billboard.com/artist/adele/

Britannica Kids: Adele
    https://kids.britannica.com/students/article/Adele/574561

Daily, Lisa. *Pop Music*. San Diego: ReferencePoint, 2020.

Grammy Awards: Adele
    https://www.grammy.com/artists/adele/528

National Geographic. *Turn It Up! A Pitch-Perfect History of Music That Rocked the World*. Washington, DC: National Geographic, 2019.

Schwartz, Heather E. *Beyoncé: The Queen of Pop*. Minneapolis: Lerner Publications, 2019.

INDEX

19, 20, 22–23, 25
21, 7–9, 19, 26, 28–29, 33
25, 34–35, 38
30, 37–38, 41

Adkins, Angelo, 31, 34–35, 37–38, 41
Adkins, Penny, 9–10, 12, 16, 19

British Record Industry Trust (BRIT)
   Awards, 29, 39, 41

"Chasing Pavements," 22–24
Columbia Records, 22–24
Cure, 10, 19

Epworth, Paul, 25, 33–34

Fitzgerald, Ella, 15

"Hello," 33–34, 41

James, Etta, 15

Konecki, Simon, 30–31, 35, 37, 41
Kurstin, Greg, 33

London, UK, 9–10, 12, 16, 18, 23, 25,
   34–35, 39, 41

Mars, Bruno, 33
Massachusetts General Hospital, 28
McCartney, Paul, 21
MySpace, 16–17

"Rolling in the Deep," 25–27
"Rumour Has It," 26

Saturday Night Live (SNL), 23
"Someone Like You," 26

Tedder, Ryan, 24–26

XL Recordings, 17–18, 22, 24